ENTERPRISE
STEM

CHILDREN'S LIBRARY

Shirley Duke

ROURKE
PUBLISHING

www.rourkepublishing.com

www.rourkepublishing.com

PHOTO CREDITS: Cover: © NASA, Andrey Armyagov, Paul Lemke, Vikram Raghuvanshi Photography; Title Page: © Michal Rózewski; Page 2: © Gregory Spencer; Page 5: © Don Bayley; Page 6: © LajosRepasi; Page 7: © Mara Radeva, mark wragg, NASA, ryasick; Page 8: © Vincent Giordano, kryczka, virtualphoto; Page 9, 10, 23: © Alexander Raths; Page 11: © NASA, Nael Nabil; Page 12: © Lisa-Joy Zgorski, National Science Foundation; Page 13, 14: © NOAA; Page 15: © NOAA, Petty Officer 3rd Class Stephen Lehmann; Page 16: © Adam Radosavljevic; Page 17: © mattasbestos, chris11; Page 18: © wavebreakmedia; Page 19: © James Herriot; Page 20: © Wikipedia: User: Alsandro, jabiru; Page 21, 39: © Christopher Futcher; Page 22: © Peter Kim; Page 24: © andres_; Page 25: © skhoward, LdF; Page 26: © s-dmit; Page 27: © exi5; Page 28: © blackwaterimages; Page 29: © studiocasper; Page 31: © Associated Press - Paul Sakuma; Page 32: © Rob Broek; Page 33: © Baris Simsek; Page 34: © Nael Nabil; Page 35: © Monika Wisniewska; Page 36: © mikeuk; Page 37: © LajosRepasi; Page 38: © vm; Page 40: © goce risteski, paci77; Page 41: © kristian sekulic, Nael Nabil; Page 42: © US Army; Page 43: © Catherine Yeulet; Page 44: © Rmarmion; Page 45: © Chris Schmidt, Nael Nabil;

Edited by Precious McKenzie

Cover design and page layout by Tara Raymo

Library of Congress Cataloging-in-Publication Data

Duke, Shirley
 Enterprise Stem / Shirley Duke.
    p. cm. -- (Let's Explore Science)
 Includes bibliographical references and index.
 ISBN 978-1-61741-781-8 (hard cover) (alk. paper)
 ISBN 978-1-61741-983-6 (soft cover)
 Library of Congress Control Number: 2011924826

Rourke Publishing
Printed in the United States of America, North Mankato, Minnesota
060711
060711CL

www.rourkepublishing.com - rourke@rourkepublishing.com
Post Office Box 643328 Vero Beach, Florida 32964

Table of Contents

CHAPTER ONE

Explaining Enterprise STEM

"I'd rather clean my room than do math."

"Taking out the garbage is more fun than science."

"You have to take the hardest subjects to be prepared for the future."

"It's important to take as much math and science as possible."

These comments came from students. Over three-fourths of U.S. students say science and math are subjects to avoid. The U.S. ranks twenty-first in science and twenty-fifth in math in the world. Yet in the next ten years, eighty percent of jobs will require people skilled in math and science.

Worldwide, Finland, China, and Australia ranked in the top five. The difference? Their students think it's important to take science and math. They say those subjects help them be successful.

Take a look around. Items that make life better come from the work of scientists, technicians, engineers, or mathematicians.

Enterprise STEM is the body of knowledge and the steps it takes to acquire that knowledge by people who work in science, technology, engineering, or mathematics. That includes **enterprise**, or the business needed to achieve a result, that goes with **research**: peer reviews, truthful reporting, and publishing results. In everyday language, it's called STEM.

People in STEM have certain qualities. Most are interested in math and science. They ask questions, are curious, and work well in teams. They use information to problem solve and to communicate effectively.

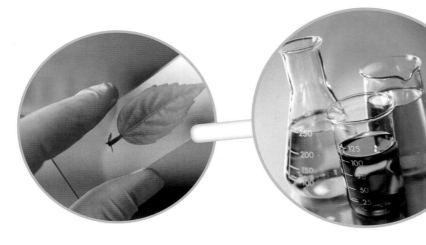

Natural science includes life and earth science. Life scientists study plants, animals, and single-celled life. Physical science studies non-living parts of the world. That's Earth, space, and the laws of nature. Technicians also work in natural sciences.

Technology involves any job with technical skills. Most often, technology means computers and programs. People use math, logic, and computer science to make computers work in systems. Others design new ways for computers to work.

Engineers use science to solve problems. They design, develop, and test new products.

The field of mathematics has people who develop ideas and create tools by using math. Some build codes that keep documents or programs safe. Others solve math problems. Statisticians calculate risks for car accidents or hurricanes. Creating math models improves how things run in factories and commerce.

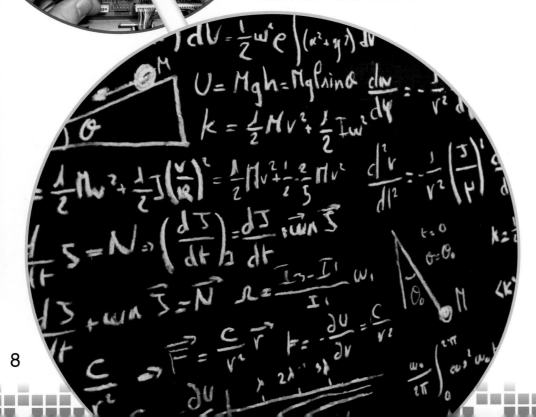

Scientists are always searching for answers to the world's questions.

Enterprise STEM is a way for young people to prepare to be competitive in a changing world. "*Educate to Innovate*" is a government program. In it, education, businesses, non-profit groups, and STEM associations will work together to help American students improve in STEM subjects.

CHAPTER TWO

STEM and Scientists at Work

Education is a big part of STEM at all levels. The STEM Education **Coalition** supports national programs for educators. The people in this group work to promote STEM education and research.

Research is a systematic investigation to learn facts. It takes place in for-profit labs, universities, businesses, and government agencies. The National Science Foundation (NSF) funds research.

Teamwork is an important part of the STEM Coalition. Without teamwork, advancements would happen at a much slower speed.

Space is often called the final frontier because there is still so much to discover.

The National Institutes of Health (NIH) do medical research. NIH supports research for treating diseases and finding cures. The National Aeronautics and Space Administration (NASA) has STEM workers collaborating to develop the space program. The Department of Energy Science Office is exploring research computer tools. The Environmental Protection Agency (EPA) works with computer software to model ecosystems for pollution studies.

What Does It Mean?

STEM: Science, Technology, Engineering, and Math

NSF: National Science Foundation

NSTA: National Science Teachers of America

ISTE: International Society for Technology in Education

SEE: Science, Engineering, and Education

NIH: National Institutes of Health

NASA: National Aeronautics and Space Administration

NOAA: National Oceanic and Atmospheric Administration

EPA: Environmental Protection Agency

NSTC: National Science and Technology Council

Universities often do their own research. Funding for the work comes from many places. Georgia Institute of Technology and Bryn Mawr College are studying ways to use personal robots in computer science.

Private companies do research for profit. The facts they learn must be something people will pay to have, such as medicines, parts for surgery, or military equipment. Often the companies work with universities, industries, or governments to keep up to date.

Jaemi, a humanoid robot (HUBO), was created by a team from Drexel University working in collaboration with Korean researchers.

People often work within their own field in STEM. Other times, the fields overlap. But disasters such as the Loma Prieta earthquake and Hurricane Katrina created a new need—earthquake and hurricane engineering.

Engineers work to make designs and structures safe in the first place. But after Hurricane Katrina, engineers, architects, insurance companies, coastal scientists, and government agencies worked as a team to rebuild the damaged areas. Engineers also worked with them to decide what caused the damage.

Engineers and scientists worked together to design new structures to protect New Orleans from future hurricanes and floodwaters.

New building codes came as a result of the work done in New Orleans. STEM workers showed the value of a new field that combines civil, wind, and structural engineering to prepare cities for storms.

Airmen from the 2nd Civil Engineer Squadron at Barksdale Air Force Base helped rebuild homes as part of Habitat for Humanity..

The Gulf oil spill brought together the National Oceanic and Atmospheric Administration (NOAA) and Gulf coast ocean and weather scientists. They monitored the spill and clean-up efforts. They worked together online and in the field. Then they published their findings.

Scientists and engineers work to learn from disasters and to prevent future disasters. They want to make our world a safer, cleaner place to live.

Does this look confusing? Analysts find this type of work interesting and fun, like trying to solve a puzzle!

Mathematics is common to all STEM subjects. Science, technology, and engineering each require math.

Math teachers use educational strategies and math. **Actuaries** analyze mathematical statistics and apply them to the fields of finance and insurance. Computer scientists use math theories and apply these theories to computers.

Biomathematics uses math techniques and tools in models, cell studies, and genetics. **Cryptography** uses math and computer science to hide information using codes. This field keeps bank accounts, credit card information, and passwords safe.

Studying math prepares students for many jobs. Math teaches people to question, explain, and use theories to solve real problems.

Example of Cryptography

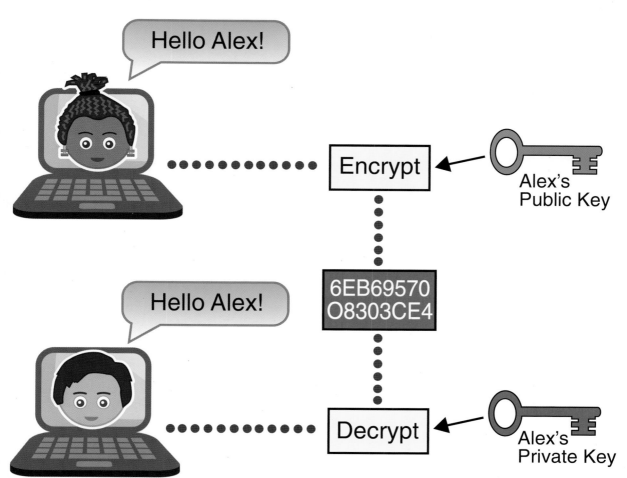

CHAPTER THREE

Working Together

Many scientists and researchers **collaborate**, or work together. They exchange documents, discuss, create, organize their work, and publish the new information. Using technology organizes their work and helps them show their results.

People read the results to learn and understand the new findings. Networking tools like wikis, blogs, Twitter, and databases help share their results, too.

18

One example of collaboration is the Human **Genome** Project. Many countries worked as a team to sequence the genetic material on human **chromosomes**.

Over 1,000 scientists worldwide worked together. They mapped the human genome by February, 2001. Technology and teamwork made it faster.

Did You Know?

They Couldn't Get Along

In the 1950s, research scientists Rosalind Franklin and Maurice Wilkins might have won the race to show DNA's structure. Working together, the strong-minded Franklin clashed with Wilkins, who treated Franklin as an assistant rather than an equal.

Wilkins went behind Franklin's back and showed Franklin's crystal X-ray to two other scientists. These two scientists, James Watson and Francis Click, did work together well. Soon after, Watson and Click knew the answer—DNA had a double spiral shape. They received credit for explaining the structure of DNA.

Architects, civil engineers, and bank owners collaborated to create a "green" office building, the Hearst Tower, in New York. This skyscraper used recycled materials, natural lighting, and wastewater collection for cooling. It set the standard for future buildings.

The Grand Canyon didn't take engineering or technology—just time and water. But the glass Skywalk, extending 70 feet (21.34 meters) over the canyon, took the collaboration of engineers, designers, construction workers, and Hualapai Indians to make it happen.

Hearst Tower is the first "green" high rise office made from recycled materials.

The glass viewing deck on Skywalk sits 4,000 feet (1,219 meters) above.

Many young scientists start their professional training at university labs before they move on to paid scientific work.

Teamwork isn't always easy. People compete for research money. Drug companies want to make a profit. Their interests may conflict with peoples' needs.

Other problems involve paperwork. Funding often requires complex applications. Filling out forms and registering new products takes time. Another problem is the amount of information. The fast pace of technology creates its own problems with sharing, storing, and keeping up with it all.

Teamwork and communication lets STEM ideas be known. Practicing teamwork from the early years prepares students to enter the STEM fields.

CHAPTER FOUR

Technology in Today's World

It's hard to imagine a time when computers, cell phones, and iPods weren't around. Technology helps improve lives in many ways.

In the early 1900s, fingerprinting placed suspects at crime scenes. But reading the pale prints often proved difficult. In 1982, Army investigators cracked a fish tank and repaired it with Superglue. They noticed their darkened prints later. Chemical fumes from the glue condensed to darken the prints. Now police regularly use the chemical.

Science has made solving crimes much more reliable than in the past.

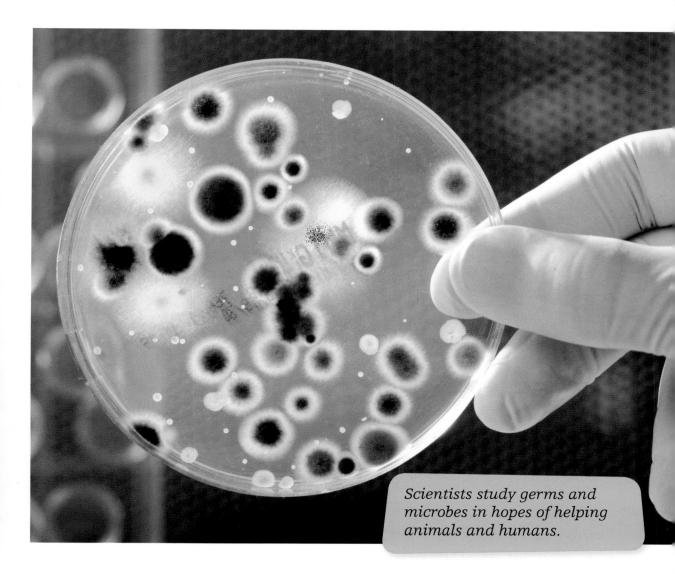

Scientists study germs and microbes in hopes of helping animals and humans.

Preventing pollution unites engineers and environmental scientists. They're working to halt medicines ending up in oceans and cleaning up waterways. **Bioremediation**, using microbes to eat up pollution like oil spills, combines science and engineering.

Other researchers monitor rain forest habitats, study tree biology, and measure climate data to improve weather predictions. Engineers work to improve hybrid and electric cars.

Satellite Transmission

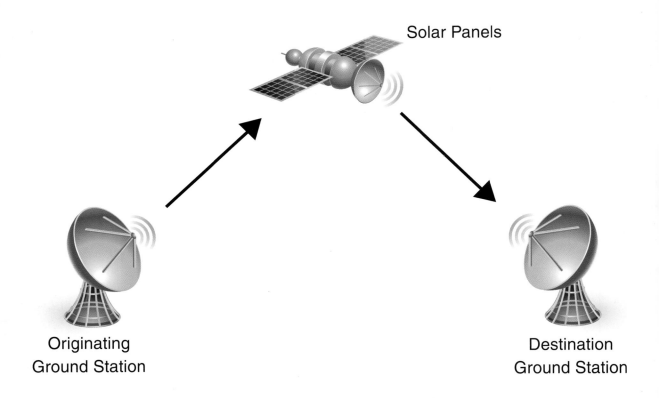

Solar Panels

Originating
Ground Station

Destination
Ground Station

Cell phones, smart phones, televisions, and GPS rely on satellite signals. Satellites make navigation possible. Weather satellites send information about the atmosphere's conditions. The military uses them for imaging and guiding missiles.

Information sharing is a major part of communication. Information sharing improves safety. Battle training simulations in the military rely on math models to create conditions for making choices. A robotic insect may be used as a spy or to detect dangerous chemicals.

Digital collections and libraries are growing. These collections take many forms. The University of Texas in Austin has an online access to its biology collections. The e-Skeletons Project lets users study the bones of a human, gorilla, and baboon digitally. The health care industry uses online chart information to keep patient records up to date. Technology creates maps of all kinds.

Did You Know?

What Time is It?

In the early 1900s, men's watches remained in their pockets until they needed to know the time. Only women wore "wristlets" as jewelry. During World War I, digging in pockets was difficult in battle. Watches held on the arm by straps proved safer. Men brought home watches after the war and soon everyone wore them on their arm. Today, people use their phones when they need to tell the time.

CHAPTER FIVE

Technology for the Future

Technology is exploding. Tools to manage search engines make it faster to gain and organize information. Data storage and programming language uses mathematics to improve communications. Virtual workspaces simplify teamwork. Images and music have been transformed into digital technology. Now digital engineering gives music its final sound.

STEM knowledge reaches everywhere to improve our daily lives. And the future promises more.

Teams of highly skilled scientists made your digital music possible!

Example of Virtual WiFi

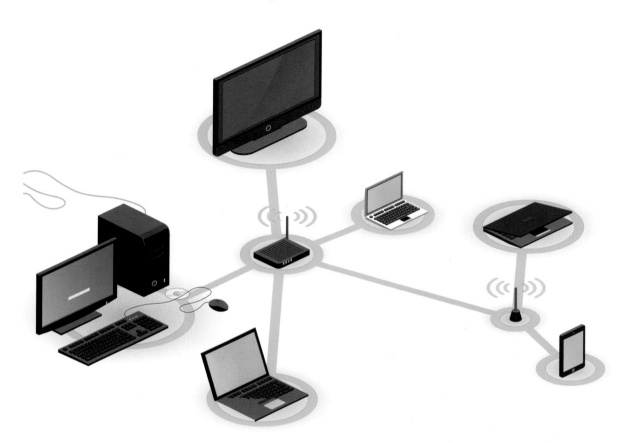

With spam blocking, **Virtual WiFi** and its multi-wireless networks, and high performance computers, technology promises amazing changes for the future.

STEM depends on computer science for research. So computer scientists search for gaps in technology and solve those problems. Each step leads to more information. Technology works to improve and manage software. Quickly finding and fixing problems with systems is critical. Researchers need good technology to organize and locate data.

Imagine something 80,000 times smaller than a human hair. Then make changes and control it. That's what **nanotechnology** does. This rapidly developing science captures and engineers tiny pieces of material with great precision. At this size, everyday matter may act differently. Much still needs to be learned in this field.

Using this technology can produce drugs, reduce emissions, and filter water. Nanoparticles are in many products, like sun block and paint. Scientists and engineers work to find practical uses and learn more so that we can improve the quality of our lives.

Some models of sunglasses use nanotechnology in the film that protects your eyes from the Sun's **ultraviolet** *rays.*

Now companies are investing in recycling computer parts so that natural resources such as gold, copper, silver, silicone, iron, and steel are not wasted.

Processing power and speeds will increase with **multi-core processors**. This technology connects two or more processors in a single unit. This provides more speed while using less power.

Others focus on the next-generation of processors. **Quantum computing** holds huge processing power by working in a single operation. It computes large amounts of data in all its states at the same time. In comparison, today's computers work with data in order instead of all at once.

Gene therapy treats diseases by changing a person's **genes** or correcting them. Cancer centers and universities work together, learning to repair faulty genes that cause cystic fibrosis, heart disease, AIDS, and cancer. Cell therapy, like a bone marrow transplant, puts whole cells into a patient to treat a disease.

Researchers are even growing new organs to replace diseased organs. They've grown rat lung tissue that works like real lungs. Berkeley engineers have created bionic eLegs to help paralyzed people walk.

Nanotechnology in chemical genetics is helping grow heart tissue and blood vessels after heart attacks. **Biomaterials** are engineered to replace body parts like bones and joints. The injected gel-like liquid creates a frame to grow cells.

Amanda Boxtel uses bionic eLegs. The crutches pick up her arm motions to signal a walking gait.

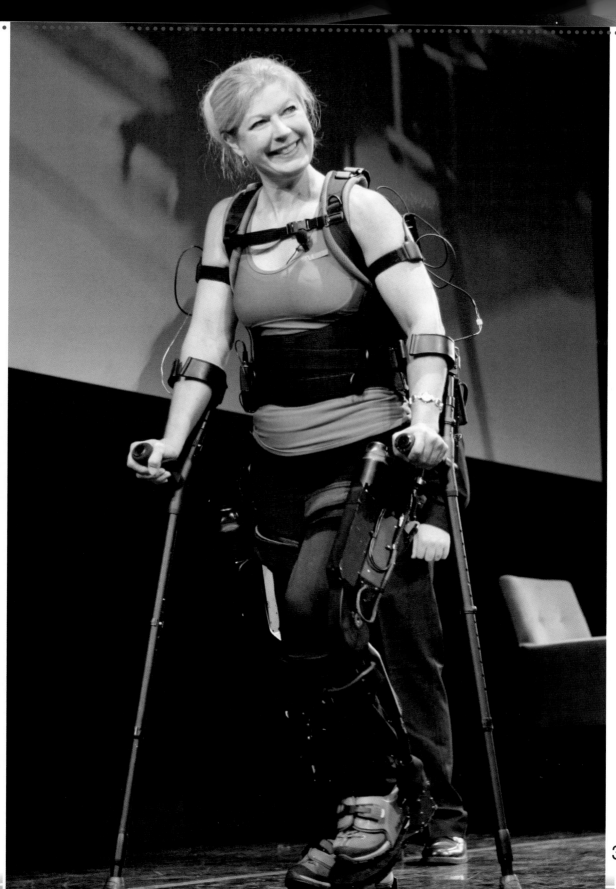

Researchers study the environment using technology. Others alter microbes to consume toxins and break them down. One modified bacterium destroys metals and oils. Nanotechnology in this microbe may be used in batteries as it converts waste into energy.

Other researchers find ways to reduce emissions and get better mileage. Hydrogen may used as fuel of the future. And biofuels—using fast growing crops and farm waste to create fuels—may join solar, wind, and geothermal power to meet energy needs.

Scientists must be very careful when they handle materials so that they do not contaminate the environment or themselves.

Advancements in special effects technology makes it difficult to distinguish fact from fiction.

Technology holds changes for entertainment, too. The Sense-Cam records images and data to create a visual blog of a person's day. A new system for capturing and storing digital photos and videos lets families record memories.

Technology has improved 3D special effects. Even NASCAR racing leads to STEM. With drivers looking for an edge, they rely on engineering.

STEM addresses problems people face. It also requires computing power, tools, and technology far beyond today's levels.

CHAPTER SIX

STEM Careers

STEM careers grow more important as technical work increases. A strong enterprise depends on the latest information. STEM provides many choices for exciting careers.

Natural science includes life science and physical science. Life scientists study living things. From basic building blocks to ecosystems, life science jobs vary. Food and agriculture scientists study production and ways to improve crop quality and safety.

Major Fields in Engineering

Aeronautics and Astronautics – all forms of flight or space

Biological engineering – making products from living things or create ways to improve life

Chemical engineering – chemistry and physics to improve industries

Civil engineering – planning for construction projects

Computer science engineering – all parts of developing computers, operating systems, and programs

Electrical and electronic engineering – power, communications

Environmental engineering – developing environment-friendly industries

Mechanical engineering – manufacturing engines, machines, and cars

Nanotechnology engineering – creating new materials from atomic-sized particles

Nuclear engineering – knowledge about nuclear energy to solve problems

Systems engineering – designing and developing large, complex systems like the ballistic missile system

Biologists study plants, animals, and bacteria. They research their lives and how they adapt. They study cells and the body's functions and actions. Geneticists study the building blocks of life and find ways to improve them. Medical scientists and researchers look for ways to prevent and treat diseases and illnesses.

Some scientific fields combine work outdoors with lab work. Conservation scientists and foresters manage natural resources. They care for renewable resources, like forests, and plan conservation efforts.

Physical scientists study the non-living world. They research space and all the matter within it. Some study the smallest particles of matter. Others study weather conditions and forecast atmospheric changes.

Chemists learn how materials act or create new kinds of materials using technology. Environmental and water scientists monitor water and air quality and check for pollutants. They find ways to protect our natural resources.

Physicists and astronomers use math to create models of how nature and its forces work. Some study energy.

Geologists explore the structure, layers, and motions of the Earth. They also help locate natural resources.

Technicians help collect specimens and analyze data.

Technology includes information technology (IT) or computer-related jobs. These careers create and improve software, databases, or computer systems. Some help people use computers and keep them running.

Researchers create programs to fit the needs of STEM careers or make computers work better.

Technicians and drafters assist engineers. They draw plans, build models, maps, and perform calculations.

Engineers use science and math to solve problems. They design, develop, and test new products. Some plan and design entire systems, like electric power grids, assembly lines, or manufacturing lines.

Most engineers specialize in civil, electrical, agricultural, biomedical, and mechanical engineering. Others study aerospace, chemical, environmental, and petroleum engineering.

In math, actuaries use statistics to calculate risks of future events. Floods, hurricanes, or car accidents are uncertain risks. The information lets insurance companies decide what kinds of insurance to offer and how much to charge.

Research analysts use math to create models that show the processes in industry, such as assembly lines or the best ways to move materials. Some jobs involve math research to solve complex problems. Finance, banking, and accounting use math.

Financial planners help people determine the best ways to invest their money and plan for retirement.

CHAPTER SEVEN

Be a Part of STEM

People must be educated in science, technology, engineering, and mathematics to remain competitive in today's world. Fewer students take math and science now. Women and minorities are under-represented in the STEM fields. It's important to change current thinking and value math and science. That starts at a young age.

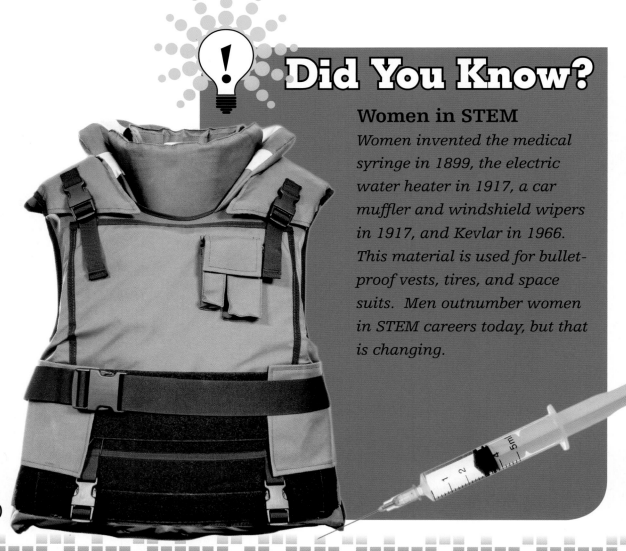

Did You Know?

Women in STEM

Women invented the medical syringe in 1899, the electric water heater in 1917, a car muffler and windshield wipers in 1917, and Kevlar in 1966. This material is used for bullet-proof vests, tires, and space suits. Men outnumber women in STEM careers today, but that is changing.

Prepare early for a STEM career. Take as much math and science as possible. Get familiar with and use technology. Talk to adults and plan for your future. Many STEM careers require a college degree. Scholarships are available, particularly for students in STEM fields.

Get involved in after-school activities that focus on problem solving skills. Science, technology, and math clubs let students explore STEM. Clubs take field trips and go to science and math competitions. Talk with school counselors about choosing STEM subjects.

Math Courses to Take in High School

Algebra 1 – subject where symbols represent numbers, stand for quantities, and show relationships.

Geometry – the properties, measurement, and relationships of points, lines, angles, surfaces, and solids.

Algebra 2 – the study of relations and functions, their graphs, and conic sections.

Trigonometry – studies triangles and the relationships between their sides and their angles.

Calculus – a complex branch of mathematics often used to study functions and limits and solve complex problems.

Statistics – science of collecting, organizing, and interpreting data.

Space Camp scholarship winners had the opportunity to create their own model rocket and train with real life scientists and astronauts.

Summer camps prepare students for STEM. Space camps provide a way to experience astronaut training. Sea camps helps kids learn about marine biology and the environment. Other camps relate to math, science, or computers. Campers may design and create their own computer games or secret codes. Some build robots, motors, or models.

Students who are curious, logical, and love to explore their ideas should think about STEM careers. Learn about the "Educate to Innovate" program.

A strong mathematics background combined with creativity and problem solving skills prepares students for careers in STEM. See what it's like to be a part of STEM!

Advances in medical technology allow people to live longer. This has caused tremendous growth in the health care field.

About 2.5 million workers will be entering a STEM career for the first time between 2004 and 2014. Computer related occupations should grow faster than most other STEM jobs. The fastest growing occupations in the next decade will be biomedical engineers, network systems and data communications analysts, and home health aides.

Companies need qualified people to work. So STEM jobs start at a pay level higher than many jobs in other fields. Computer software engineers have the highest median pay rate.

Funding for research in the sciences supports STEM subjects. The STEM Coalition is working to raise standards for U.S. education.

Quality teachers improve STEM learning so governors of all fifty states have come together to encourage STEM education. Innovations solve problems and make the economy strong.

People who can create and develop new ideas and products in enterprise STEM will direct the future.

STEM Organizations

American Design Drafting Association
www.adda.org

American Society for Engineering Education
www.asee.org

Junior Engineering Technical Society
www.jets.org

American Mathematical Society
www.ams.org/employment

Mathematical Association of America
www.maa.org

Society for Industrial and Applied Mathematics
www.siam.org/students

American Association for the Advancement of Science
www.aaas.org/

Association of Information Technology Professionals
www.aitp.org/

Glossary

actuaries (ak-CHOO-air-eez): people who compute insurance risks and set policy amounts using statistics

biomaterials (BYE-oh-muh-TEER-ee-uhlz): medical materials used to replace or allow normal tissue to regrow

biomathematics (bye-oh-math-uh-MAY-iks): using math techniques and tools in the study of life science, such as models, cell studies, or genetics

bioremediation (bye-oh-ri-MEE-dee-a-shun): using microbes to clean up environmental damage or hazards

chromosomes (KROH-muh-sohmz): structure that carries the genetic information inside a cell's nucleus

coalition (koh-uh-lish-uhn): a group working together toward a common goal

collaborate (kuh-ILAB-uh-rate): to work together on a project or activity

cryptography (krip-TAH-gruh-fee): using math and computer science code to hide information

enterprise (EN-tur-prize): a plan to do something in steps leading to a result that often takes place in businesses

Enterprise STEM (EN-tur-prize stem): the body of knowledge and the steps taken to acquire that knowledge by people who work in science, technology, engineering, or mathematics

genes (jeenz): a tiny unit that carries the code for inherited traits in chromosomes

genome (JEE-nohm): the complete set of chromosomes in a living thing

multi-core processors (MUHL-ti- kor PRAH-ses-urz): two or more processors connected working as a single system to increase its power

nanotechnology (nan-oh-tek-NAH-luh-jee): technology able to capture and manage tiny pieces of material with extreme precision

quantum computing (KWAHN-tum kuhm-PYOO-ting): a computer unit that works on multiple levels at the same time so that a single operation acts on great amounts of data, increasing power and reducing energy use

research (ri-SURCH): a systematic investigation to learn facts

ultraviolet (uhl-truh-VYE-uh-lit): a kind of light wave that can't be seen but kills microbes and tans skin

Virtual WiFi (VUR-choo-uhl-wye-fye): using a single wireless card to move between many wireless networks, making the users feel they are connected to many wireless networks at the same time

Index

Websites to Visit

www.smithsonianeducation.org/students/

www.girlsgotech.org/girlsgotech_booklet.pdf

www.apples4theteacher.com/math.html

www.nasa.gov/audience/forstudents/

About the Author

Shirley Duke enjoys science and books. She studied biology and education at Austin College in Texas. Then she taught science in elementary, middle, and high school for many years. Using her science background, she changed careers and now writes books for young people, thanks to her STEM background. In addition to a picture book and a young adult book, her first two science books are in the Let's Explore Science series. Visit Shirley at www.shirleysmithduke.com or www.simplyscience.wordpress.com.